LET US COMPARE
MYTHOLOGIES

BY LEONARD COHEN

FICTION
The Favourite Game *(1963)*
Beautiful Losers *(1966)*

POETRY
Let Us Compare Mythologies *(1956)*
The Spice-Box of Earth *(1961)*
Flowers for Hitler *(1964)*
Parasites of Heaven *(1966)*
Selected Poems, 1956-1968 *(1968)*
The Energy of Slaves *(1972)*
Death of a Lady's Man *(1978)*
Book of Mercy *(1984)*
Stranger Music: Selected Poems and Songs *(1993)*
Book of Longing *(2006)*

ALBUMS
Songs of Leonard Cohen *(1967)*
Songs from a Room *(1969)*
Songs of Love and Hate *(1971)*
Live Songs *(1972)*
New Skin for the Old Ceremony *(1973)*
The Best of Leonard Cohen *(1975)*
Death of a Ladies' Man *(1977)*
Recent Songs *(1979)*
Various Positions *(1984)*
I'm Your Man *(1988)*
The Future *(1992)*
Cohen Live *(1994)*
More Best of Leonard Cohen *(1997)*
Field Commander Cohen *(2001)*
Ten New Songs *(2001)*
The Essential Leonard Cohen *(2002)*
Dear Heather *(2004)*

LET US COMPARE MYTHOLOGIES

by Leonard Cohen

Drawings by Freda Guttman

An Imprint of HarperCollins*Publishers*

HarperCollins books may be purchased for educational, business, or sales
promotional use. For information, please e-mail the Special Markets
Department at SPsales@harpercollins.com.

First published in Canada in 1956 for the McGill Poetry Series by
Contact Press, Toronto.

Published by McClelland and Stewart in 1966.

First Ecco edition published in 2007.

Library of Congress Cataloging-in-Publication Data is
available upon request.

ISBN: 978-0-06117375-2
ISBN-10: 0-06-117375-4

22 23 24 25 26 LBC 15 14 13 12 11

To the memory of my father

Nathan B. Cohen

'All right,' he said. 'Listen,' and read again, but only one stanza this time and closed the book and laid it on the table. 'She cannot fade, though thou hast not thy bliss,' McCaslin said: 'Forever wilt thou love, and she be fair.'

'He's talking about a girl,' he said.

'He had to talk about something,' McCaslin said.

The Bear,

by William Faulkner

CONTENTS

LET US COMPARE
MYTHOLOGIES

ELEGY

Do not look for him
In brittle mountain streams:
They are too cold for any god;
And do not examine the angry rivers
For shreds of his soft body
Or turn the shore stones for his blood;
But in the warm salt ocean
He is descending through cliffs
Of slow green water
And the hovering coloured fish
Kiss his snow-bruised body
And build their secret nests
In his fluttering winding-sheet.

FOR WILF AND HIS HOUSE

When young the Christians told me
how we pinned Jesus
like a lovely butterfly against the wood,
and I wept beside paintings of Calvary
at velvet wounds
and delicate twisted feet.

But he could not hang softly long,
your fighters so proud with bugles,
bending flowers with their silver stain,
and when I faced the Ark for counting,
trembling underneath the burning oil,
the meadow of running flesh turned sour
and I kissed away my gentle teachers,
warned my younger brothers.

Among the young and turning-great
of the large nations, innocent
of the spiked wish and the bright crusade,
there I could sing my heathen tears
between the summersaults and chestnut battles,
love the distant saint
who fed his arm to flies,
mourn the crushed ant
and despise the reason of the heel.

Raging and weeping are left on the early road.
Now each in his holy hill
the glittering and hurting days are almost done.
        Then let us compare mythologies.
I have learned my elaborate lie
of soaring crosses and poisoned thorns
and how my fathers nailed him
like a bat against a barn
to greet the autumn and late hungry ravens
as a hollow yellow sign.

THE SONG OF THE HELLENIST
(For R.K.)

*Those unshadowed figures, rounded lines of men
who kneel by curling waves, amused by ornate birds—
If that had been the ruling way,
I would have grown long hairs for the corners of my
mouth . . .*

O cities of the Decapolis across the Jordan,
you are too great; our young men love you,
and men in high places have caused gymnasiums
to be built in Jerusalem.
  I tell you, my people, the statues are too tall.
  Beside them we are small and ugly,
  blemishes on the pedestal.

My name is Theodotus, do not call me Jonathan.
My name is Dositheus, do not call me Nathaniel.
  Call us Alexander, Demetrius, Nicanor . . .

'Have you seen my landsmen in the museums,
the brilliant scholars with the dirty fingernails,
standing before the marble gods,
  underneath the lot?'
Among straight noses, natural and carved,
I have said my clever things thought out before;
jested on the Protocols, the cause of war,
  quoted 'Bleistein with a Cigar.'

— 18 —

And in the salon that holds the city in its great
                              window,
in the salon among the Herrenmenschen,
among the close-haired youth, I made them laugh
when the child came in:
    'Come I need you for a Passover Cake.'
And I have touched their tall clean women,
thinking somehow they are unclean,
    as scaleless fish.
They have smiled quietly at me,
and with their friends —
    I wonder what they see.

O cities of the Decapolis,
call us Alexander, Demetrius, Nicanor ...
    Dark women, soon I will not love you.
My children will boast of their ancestors at
                              Marathon
and under the walls of Troy,
    and Athens, my chiefest joy —

O call me Alexander, Demetrius, Nicanor ...

PRAYER FOR MESSIAH

His blood on my arm is warm as a bird
his heart in my hand is heavy as lead
his eyes through my eyes shine brighter than love
O send out the raven ahead of the dove

His life in my mouth is less than a man
his death on my breast is harder than stone
his eyes through my eyes shine brighter than love
O send out the raven ahead of the dove

O send out the raven ahead of the dove
O sing from your chains where you're chained in
                                        a cave
your eyes through my eyes shine brighter than
                                        love
your blood in my ballad collapses the grave

O sing from your chains where you're chained in
                                    a cave
your eyes through my eyes shine brighter than love
your heart in my hand is heavy as lead
your blood on my arm is warm as a bird

O break from your branches a green branch of love
after the raven has died for the dove

RITES

Bearing gifts of flowers and sweet nuts
the family came to watch the eldest son,
my father; and stood about his bed
while he lay on a blood-sopped pillow,
his heart half rotted
and his throat dry with regret.
And it seemed so obvious, the smell so present,
quiet so necessary,
but my uncles prophesied wildly,
promising life like frantic oracles;
and they only stopped in the morning,
after he had died
and I had begun to shout.

REDEDICATION

A painful rededication, this Spring,
like the building of cathedrals between wars,
and masons at decayed walls;
and we are almost too tired to begin again
with miracles and leaves
and lingering on steps in sudden sun;

tired by the way isolated drifts lie melting,
like hulks of large fish rotting far upbeach;
the disinterested scrape of shovels
collecting sand from sidewalks, destroying streams;
and school-children in streetcars,
staring out, astonished.

We had learned a dignity in late winter,
from austere trees and dry brown bushes,
but Spring disturbs us like the morning,
and we may hope only for no October.

PIONEERS

After one furious year
you thought you could come back
with singing armies,
to cheer the landscape
and startle old streams.
But someone's bulldozers
had heaved the river aside
and fish screamed against fossils
in the drying sand.

Because you learned
some family lines in faces
and let go gratefully
the easy silhouettes,
did you believe
the treacherous dead year
could go quiet and unmourned
and leave no time
for gasping and for breath?

So roar with your comrades
in the staggering mountains,
or weep with them
at high views of coloured water.
But nourish the tired saplings
with your marking axe,
and if your swing draws blood,
dig deeper,
and the autumn path
will not seem so intricate.

THE SPARROWS

Catching winter in their carved nostrils
the traitor birds have deserted us,
leaving only the dullest brown sparrows
for spring negotiations.

I told you we were fools
to have them in our games,
but you replied:
        They are only wind-up birds
who strut on scarlet feet
so hopelessly far
from our curled fingers.

I had moved to warn you,
but you only adjusted your hair
and ventured:
        Their wings are made of glass and gold
and we are fortunate
not to hear them splintering
against the sun.

Now the hollow nests
sit like tumors or petrified blossoms
between the wire branches
and you, an innocent scientist,
question me on these brown sparrows:
whether we should plant
                              our yards with breadcrumbs
or mark them with the black, persistent crows
whom we hate and stone.

But what shall I tell you of migrations
when in this empty sky
the precise ghosts of departed summer birds
still trace old signs;
or of desperate flights
when the dimmest flutter of a coloured wing
excites all our favourite streets
to delight in imaginary spring.

ITEM

Let the still-born eagle demonstrate
how he avoided the arrow
with it's predicament of death: his closed eyes,
his half-formed feathers.
Let him teach how wise
was his early death, how the hunter
paused only a moment in the narrow path
and would not waste his arm
to cool the quick dying warmth.

And let the heroes with their promised swords
consider the darker battle:
the unthinking steel, the old but difficult flesh,
the thrust and the regret.
And let them speculate
on their chipped skeletons
moving on the dry field of death,
how very painful and loud and brittle.
Then let them remember the still-born eagle
and the young bird bones which do not hurt or
rattle.

CITY CHRIST

He has returned from countless wars,
Blinded and hopelessly lame.
He endures the morning streetcars
And counts ages in a Peel Street room.

He is kept in his place like a court jew,
To consult on plagues or hurricanes,
And he never walks with them on the sea
Or joins their lonely sidewalk games.

SONG OF PATIENCE

For a lovely instant I thought she would grow mad
and end the reason's fever.
but in her hand she held Christ's splinter,
so I could only laugh and press a warm coin
across her seasoned breasts:
but I remembered clearly then your insane letters
and how you wove initials in my throat.

My friends warn me
that you have read the oceans's old skeleton;
they say you stitch the water sounds
in different mouths, in other monuments.
'Journey with a silver bullet,' they caution.
'Conceal a stake inside your pocket.'
And I must smile as they misconstrue your insane
                                    letters

and my embroidered throat.

O I will tell him to love you carefully;
to honour you with shells and coloured bottles;
to keep from your face the falling sand
and from your human arm the time-charred
                                    beetle;

to teach you new stories about lightning
and let you run sometimes barefoot on the shore.
And when the needle grins bloodlessly in his cheek
he will come to know how beautiful it is
to be loved by a madwoman.

And I do not gladly wait the years
for the ocean to discover and rust your face
as it has all of history's beacons
that have turned their gold and stone to water's
                                        onslaught,
for then your letters too rot with ocean's logic
and my fingernails are long enough
to tear the stitches from my throat.

WHEN THIS AMERICAN WOMAN

When this American woman,
whose thighs are bound in casual red cloth,
comes thundering past my sitting-place
like a forest-burning Mongol tribe,
the city is ravished
and brittle buildings of a hundred years
splash into the street;
and my eyes are burnt
for the embroidered Chinese girls,
already old,
and so small between the thin pines
on these enormous landscapes,
that if you turn your head
they are lost for hours.

THESE HEROICS

If I had a shining head
and people turned to stare at me
in the street cars;
and I could stretch my body
through the bright water
and keep abreast of fish and water snakes;
if I could ruin my feathers
in flight before the sun;
do you think that I would remain in this room,
reciting poems to you,
and making outrageous dreams
with the smallest movements of your mouth?

SONG

The naked weeping girl
is thinking of my name
turning my bronze name
over and over
with the thousand fingers
of her body
anointing her shoulders
with the remembered odour
of my skin

O I am the general
in her history
over the fields
driving the great horses
dressed in gold cloth
wind on my breastplate
sun in my belly

May soft birds
soft as a story to her eyes
protect her face
from my enemies
and vicious birds
whose sharp wings
were forged in metal oceans
guard her room
from my assasins

And night deal gently with her
high stars maintain the whiteness
of her uncovered flesh

And may my bronze name
touch always her thousand fingers
grow brighter with her weeping
until I am fixed like a galaxy
and memorized
in her secret and fragile skies.

FOLK SONG

The ancient craftsman smiled
    when I asked him to blow a bottle
    to keep your tears in.
And he smiled and hummed in rhythm with his
                                 hands
    as he carved delicate glass
    and stained it with the purple
    of a drifting evening sky.
But the bottle is lost in a corner of my house.
How could I know you could not cry?

FRIENDS

The river confronted us, the Charles, and through its secret undulations swarmed the shadows of ten dozen streetlamps and a moon. Here and here, stone bridges clasped the banks and held the water like segments of a bruised worm. And we, small as Chinese mystics in a swirl of landscape, confused the light with our pebbles, broke it into spirals. That. Perhaps it was a water rat, perhaps a water snake, a small Welsh water monster that forgot the freedom of the circle and dragged an uncertain line behind it to the other side. It was a chipmunk, as we preferred, and held off the rocks.
Then I and Chen argued tenderly, he with cool faith and I with passion, until we could only speak, until we could only agree. Chen is away and writes me now, the young authentic; writes and tells me of white Theodore, and Irwin who sculptured us all in white marble.

THE WARRIOR BOATS

The warrior boats from Portugal
Strain at piers with ribs exposed
And seagull generations fall
Through the wood anatomy

But in the town, the town
Their passion unimpaired
The beautiful dead crewmen
Go climbing in the lanes
Boasting poems and bitten coins

Handsome bastards
What do they care
If the Empire has withered
To half a peninsula
If the Queen has the King's Adviser
For her last and seventh lover

Their maps have not changed
Thighs still are white and warm
New boundaries have not altered
The marvellous landscape of bosoms
Nor a Congress relegated the red mouth
To a foreign district

Then let the ships disintegrate
At the edge of the land
The gulls will find another place to die
Let the home ports put on mourning
And little clerks
Complete the necessary papers

But you swagger on, my enemy sailors
Go climbing in the lanes
Boasting your poems and bitten coins
Go knocking on all the windows of the town

At one place you will find my love
Asleep and waiting
And I cannot know how long
She has dreamed of all of you

Oh remove my coat gently
From her shoulders.

LOVERS

During the first pogrom they
Met behind the ruins of their homes —
Sweet merchants trading: her love
For a history-full of poems.

And at the hot ovens they
Cunningly managed a brief
Kiss before the soldier came
To knock out her golden teeth.

And in the furnace itself
As the flames flamed higher,
He tried to kiss her burning breasts
As she burned in the fire.

Later he often wondered:
Was their barter completed?
While men around him plundered
And knew he had been cheated.

SONG

My lover Peterson
He named me Goldenmouth
I changed him to a bird
And he migrated south

My lover Frederick
Wrote sonnets to my breast
I changed him to a horse
And he galloped west

My lover Levite
He named me Bitterfeast
I changed him to a serpent
And he wriggled east

My lover I forget
He named me Death
I changed him to a catfish
And he swam north

My lover I imagine
He cannot form a name
I'll nestle in his fur
And never be to blame.

LETTER

How you murdered your family
means nothing to me
as your mouth moves across my body

And I know your dreams
of crumbling cities and galloping horses
of the sun coming too close
and the night never ending

but these mean nothing to me
beside your body

I know that outside a war is raging
that you issue orders
that babies are smothered and generals beheaded

but blood means nothing to me
it does not disturb your flesh

tasting blood on your tongue
does not shock me
as my arms grow into your hair

Do not think I do not understand
what happens
after the troops have been massacred
and the harlots put to the sword

And I write this only to rob you

that when one morning my head
hangs dripping with the other generals
from your house gate

that all this was anticipated
and so you will know that it meant nothing to me.

PAGANS

With all Greek heroes
swarming around my shoulders,
I perverted the Golem formula
and fashioned you from grass,
using oaths of cruel children
for my father's chant.

O pass by, I challenged you
and gods in their approval
rustled my hair with marble hands,
and you approached slowly
with all the pain of a thousand year statue
breaking into life.

I thought you perished
    at our first touch
(for in my hand I held a fragment
of a French cathedral
and in the air a man spoke to birds
and everywhere
the dangerous smell of old Italian flesh).

But yesterday while children
slew each other in a dozen games,
I heard you wandering through grass
and watched you glare (O Dante)
where I had stood.

I know how our coarse grass
mutilates your feet,
    how the city traffic
echoes all his sonnets
and how you lean for hours
at the cemetery gates.

Dear friend, I have searched all night
    through each burnt paper,
but I fear I will never find
the formula to let you die.

BALLAD

He pulled a flower
out of the moss
and struggled past soldiers
to stand at the cross.

He dipped the flower
into a wound
and hoped that a garden
would grow in his hand.

The hanging man shivered
at this gentle thrust
and ripped his flesh
from the flowers touch,

and said in a voice
they had not heard,
'Will petals find roots
in the wounds where I bleed?

'Will minstrels learn songs
from a tongue which is torn
and sick be made whole
through rents in my skin'?

The people knew something
like a god had spoken
and stared with fear
at the nails they had driven.

And they fell on the man
with spear and knife
to honour the voice
with a sacrifice.

O the hanging man
had words for the crowd
but he was tired
and the prayers were loud.

He thought of islands
alone in the sea
and sea water bathing
dark roots of each tree;

of tidal waves lunging
over the land,
over these crosses
these hills and this man.

He thought of towns
and fields of wheat,
of men and this man
but he could not speak.

O they hid two bodies
behind a stone;
day became night
and the crowd went home.

And men from Golgotha
assure me that still
gardeners in vain
pour blood in that soil.

PRAYER FOR SUNSET

The sun is tangled
 in black branches,
raving like Absalom
 between sky and water,
struggling through the dark terebinth
to commit its daily suicide.

Now, slowly, the sea consumes it,
leaving a glistening wound
 on the water,
 a red scar on the horizon;
In darkness
 I set out for home,
terrified by the clash of wind on grass,
and the victory cry of weeds and water.

Is there no Joab for tomorrow night,
 with three darts
 and a great heap of stones?

SAINT CATHERINE STREET

Towering black nuns frighten us
as they come lumbering down the tramway aisle
amulets and talismans caught in careful fingers
promising plagues for an imprudent glance
So we bow our places away
     the price of an indulgence

How may we be saints and live in golden coffins
Who will leave on our stone shelves
     pathetic notes for intervention
How may we be calm marble gods at ocean altars
Who will murder us for some high reason

There are no ordeals
Fire and water have passed from the wizards' hands
We cannot torture or be tortured
Our eyes are worthless to an inquisitor's heel
No prince will waste hot lead
     or build a spiked casket for us

Once with a flaming belly she danced upon a green
                           road
Move your hand slowly through a cobweb
     and make drifting strings for puppets
Now the tambourines are dull
at her lifted skirt boys study cigarette stubs
no one is jealous of her body

We would bathe in a free river
but the lepers in some spiteful gesture
have suicided in the water
and all the swollen quiet bodies crowd the other
    prey for a fearless thief or beggar

How can we love and pray
when at our lovers' arms
we hear the damp bells of them
who once took bitter alms
but now float quietly away

Will no one carve from our bodies a white cross
for a wind-torn mountain
or was that forsaken man's pain
enough to end all passion

Are those dry faces and hands we see
all the flesh there is of nuns
Are they really clever non-excreting tapestries
prepared by skillful eunuchs
for our trembling friends.

BALLAD

My lady was found mutilated
in a Mountain Street boarding house.
My lady was a tall slender love,
        like one of Tennyson's girls,
and you always imagined her erect on a throughbred
in someone's private forest.
        But there she was,
naked on an old bed, knife slashes
across her breasts, legs badly cut up:
Dead two days.

They promised me an early conviction.
We will eavesdrop on the adolescents
        examining pocket-book covers in drugstores.
We will note the broadest smiles at torture scenes
        in movie houses.
We will watch the old men in Dominion Square
        follow with their eyes
the secretaries from the Sun Life at five-thirty . . .

Perhaps the tabloids alarmed him.
Whoever he was the young man came alone
        to see the frightened blonde have her blouse
ripped away by anonymous hands;
the person guarded his mouth
        who saw the poker blacken the eyes
of the Roman prisoner;
the old man pretended to wind his pocket-watch . . .

The man was never discovered.
There are so many cities!
    so many knew of my lady and her beauty.
Perhaps he came from Toronto, a half-crazed man
    looking for some Sunday love;
or a vicious poet stranded too long in Winnipeg;
or a Nova Scotian fleeing from the rocks and
                                    preachers...

Everyone knew my lady
    from the movies and art-galleries,
Body by Goldwyn. Botticelli had drawn her long
                                    limbs.
Rossetti the full mouth.
Ingres had coloured her skin.
    She should not have walked so bravely
through the streets.
After all, that was the Marian year, the year
the rabbis emerged from their desert exile, the year
the people were inflamed by tooth-paste ads ...

We buried her in Spring-time.
    The sparrows in the air
wept that we should hide with earth
    the face of one so fair.

The flowers they were roses
    and such sweet fragrance gave
that all my friends were lovers
    and we danced upon her grave.

SUMMER NIGHT

The moon dangling wet like a half-plucked eye
was bright for my friends bred in close avenues
of stone, and let us see too much.
The vast treeless field and huge wounded sky,
opposing each other like continents,
made us and our smoking fire quite irrelevant
between their eternal attitudes.
We knew we were intruders. Worse. Intruders
unnoticed and undespised.
        Through orchards of black weeds
with a sigh the river urged its silver flesh.
From their damp nests bull-frogs croaked
warnings, but to each other.
And occasional birds, in a private grudge,
flew noiselessly at the moon.
What could we do? We ran naked into the river,
but our flesh insulted the thick slow water.
We tried to sit naked on the stones,
but they were cold and we soon dressed.
One squeezed a little human music from his box:
mostly it was lost in the grass
where one struggled in an ignorant embrace.
One argued with the slight old hills
and the goose-fleshed naked girls, I will not be old.
One, for his protest, registered a sexual groan.

And the girl in my arms
broke suddenly away, and shouted for us all,
Help! Help! I am alone. But then all subtlety was
                                    gone
and it was stupid to be obvious before the field and
                                    sky,
experts in simplicity. So we fled on the highways,
in our armoured cars, back to air-conditioned
                                    homes.

THE FLIER

Do not arrange your bright flesh in the sun
Or shine your limbs, my love, toward this height
Where basket men and the lame must run, must
                                      run
And grasp at angels in their lovely flight
With stumps and hooks and artificial skin.
O there is nothing in your body's light
To grow us wings or teach the discipline
Which starvers know to calm the appetite.
Understand we might be content to beg
The clinic of your thighs against the night
Were there no scars of braces on his leg
Who sings and wrestles with them in our sight,
Then climbs the sky, a lover in their band.
Tell him your warmth, show him your gleaming
                                      hand.

HAD WE NOTHING TO PROVE

Had we nothing to prove but love
we might have leaned all night at that window,
merely beside each other,
watching Peel Street, wrought-iron gates
and weather vanes, black lace of trees
between cautious Victorian silhouettes;
     but there were obligations, the formalities
of passion; so we sealed the shutters
and were expedient in the brevity of night;
reading with empty sockets moonlight in dull hair,
softness to chafed thighs;
     both of us anxious and shaking the night,
with all my arm, she with fingers and gentle;
no hope for silver leaves in the morning.
     And always a glance for the brightening
                          window,
a suspension of breath for the hearing of birds
and incantations to the sun
which stirs in dust behind stone horizons.

SATAN IN WESTMOUNT

One noticed his hands,
finely carved,
almost the colour of jade,
and the fingernails,
pink and cultivated.
 He spoke of Art
 and of poetry
 and held us with descriptions
 of the Masters.
Often when walking
he sang fragments
of austere Spanish songs
from the Court of Ferdinand,
and quoted Dante
accurately and often.
 But in his lapel,
 discreetly,
 he wore a sprig of asphodel.

FRAGMENT OF BAROQUE

Schloss-Monbijou before the war . . .
    in a Baroque castle
        among genii, angels, stucco and tin,
she sat before a harpsichord,
    beside a candelabra
    in a dim room
playing the Couperin
    of heavy carpets and roses
    carved in wooden tables,
while the men and women
    clinging sadly to a myth
    sipped brandy
listened to the mass
    of needlework tone
and thought
    of white lace and silk fans
        soaking in river foam.

Quiet days for some,
    measured by the subtle ring of crystal
        and nods of ivory heads;
days of listening,
    of women's tongues tasting,
    of harpsicords treasured
        by Prussian queens.

TWILIGHT

Those days were just the twilight
And soon the poems and the songs
Were only associations
Edged with bitterness
Focussed into pain
By paintings in a minor key
Remembered on warm nights
When he made love to strangers
And he would struggle through old words
Unable to forget he once created new ones
And fumble at their breasts with broken hands

When finally he did become very old
And nights were cold because
No one was a stranger
And there was little to do
But sift the years through his yellow fingers
Then like fire-twisted shadows of dancers
Alternatives would array themselves
Around his wicker chair
And he regretted everything

TO I.P.L.

No answers in your delightful
zarathustrian tales,
how the streets and alleys of heaven
were not safe for holy girls,
and a century of curfew had
driven the seraphim indoors,
while He raged, depraved,
hanging around street corners,
entertaining hags in public places,
going wild with thunder and stray children;
and how you finally came in,
more furious than any Canadian poet,
and found Him gasping against a cloud,
His back already broken by some rebel band,
and not hesitating you finished up the job
while He mumbled tired curses
and a chorus of invalid angels
rattled their fists
and chanted odes to you.

HALLOWEEN POEM

Impassive frogs, skins stretched taut,
grey with late October,
the houses down my street
crouched, unaware of each other.

Unaware of a significant wind
and mad children igniting heaps of rattling leaves
and the desperate cry of desperate birds.

I don't know where the children got the birds.
Certainly, there are few around my house. Oh,
there is the occasional sparrow or robin or wren,
but these were big birds. There were several turns
of parcel twine about each bird to secure its wings
and feet. It was that particularly hard variety of
twine that can't be pulled apart but requires a
knife or scissors to be cut. I was so lost in the
ritual that I'm not sure if it was seven or eight they
burnt.

("The effluvia of festering bodies was so great
that even the Mongols avoided such places and
named them Moubaligh, City of Woe.")

Soon they grew tired of the dance
and removed their crepe-paper costumes
and said prayers and made laments.

(Now that I think about it, the birds
must have been pigeons.)

It was a quarter-to-nine
when one bright youngster
incited the group to burn the frogs,
which they did at nine.

If one of Temugin's warriors
trapped a deer to eat.
it was forbidden
to slit its throat.
The beast must be bound
and the beast's chest opened
and the heart removed
by the hunter's hand.

POEM

I heard of a man
who says words so beautifully
that if he only speaks their name
women give themselves to him.

If I am dumb beside your body
while silence blossoms like tumors on our lips
it is because I hear a man climb stairs
and clear his throat outside our door.

ON CERTAIN INCREDIBLE NIGHTS

On certain incredible nights,
When your flesh is drenched with moon
And the windows are wide open:
Your breasts are sculptured
From the soft inside of darkness
And your belly a fragment of a great bright flask.
Thank-God a peninsula of sheet across your waist
Imprisons you upon my bed.
O not toward the glory
Of the beautifully infested outside skies,
Where girls of light are floating up from every room,
Would I a moment turn my head,
As other men have innocently done!

JINGLE

To show the fat brain
rotting like stumps of brown teeth
in an old bright throat
is the final clever thrill
of summer lads all dead with love.

So here is mine,
torn and stretched for the sun,
to be used for a drum or a tambourine,
to be scratched with poetry
by Kafka's machine.

THE FLY

In his black armour
    the house-fly marched the field
of Freia's sleeping thighs,
undisturbed by the soft hand
    which vaguely moved
to end his exercise.

And it ruined my day —
    this fly which never planned
to charm her or to please
should walk boldly on that ground
    I tried so hard
to lay my trembling knees.

WARNING

If your neighbour disappears
O if your neighbour disappears
The quiet man who raked his lawn
The girl who always took the sun

Never mention it to your wife
Never say at dinner time
Whatever happened to that man
Who used to rake his lawn

Never say to your daughter
As you're walking home from church
Funny thing about that girl
I haven't seen her for a month

And if your son says to you
Nobody lives next door
They've all gone away
Send him to bed with no supper

Because it can spread, it can spread
And one fine evening coming home
Your wife and daughter and son
They'll have caught the idea and will be gone.

LES VIEUX

Northeastern Lunch,
    with rotting noses and tweed caps,
huddling in thick coats
and mumbling confidential songs
to ancient friends —
    the public men of Montreal;

and in parks
    with strange children
who listen to sad lies
in exchange for whistles
    carved from wet maple branches;

in Phillips Square,
    on newspaper-covered benches,
unaware of Ste. Catherine Street
or grey and green pigeons
    inquiring between their boots —

public men,
    letters of reference crumbling in wallets,
speaking all the languages of Montreal.

STORY

She tells me a child built her house
one Spring afternoon,
but that the child was killed
crossing the street.

She says she read it in the newspaper,
that at the corner of this and this avenue
a child was run down by an automobile.

Of course I do not believe her.
She has built the house herself,
hung the oranges and coloured beads in the
                                    doorways,
crayoned flowers on the walls.
She has made the paper things for the wind,
collected crooked stones for their shadows in the
                                    sun,
fastened yellow and dark balloons to the ceiling.

Each time I visit her
she repeats the story of the child to me,
I never question her. It is important
to understand one's part in a legend.

I take my place
among the paper fish and make-believe clocks,
naming the flowers she has drawn,
smiling while she paints my head on large clay
                                        coins,
and making a sort of courtly love to her
when she contemplates her own traffic death.

'JUST THE WORST TIME'

This year time was long between
    old gardeners tending
    black-yellow heaps of smouldering leaves
and glowing children
armoured in Red River coats and muffler-turns —
    and so as nude girls discovered bathing,
    stricken, somehow unable to cover their breasts
the embarrassed trees fidgeted
in unsolicited sun.

We were embarrassed too,
prayed for great heavy drifts of snow
to cover trees and bare streets,
to heap on roofs of houses,
to swaddle mountains and waters —

but the snow came thin,
covering the ground like cheap gauze,
clinging in tatters to the bark,
    preserving footprints in the mud.

No. It could not come like an aristocrat,
like de Bergerac,
like a white waving plume,
    as we prayed for
    and will pray for again.

SAVIORS

The Roman sport of crucifixion
casts across the lands and oceans
an old heavy shadow
which has grown into all the graves

In the valleys men review
their people's documents
and parties are dispatched to find
this heap of stones and this cave and this pillar

And dead heroes are raised on wood
above their discovered tombs
to rehearse their ancient arguments

Nailed high on a mountain
Moses stares beyond the Jordan
beyond the giants and crumbling walls
and sighs an Egyptian curse

Job hangs in a burnt field
unable to frighten the crows
his friends still talking at his feet
and no whirlwind disturbs the quiet desolation

David swings from his roof
and the people say that in his mind
he and his warriors build a great temple

And all the saints and prophets
are nailed to stakes and desert trees
All the Kings and men of ages
with deathless words and singing harps
are exhumed to die again in the wilderness

See whom they bring us today
bearing him triumphantly through the traffic
singing before his death
O he will love us O he will approve of us

See how the temple girls scent their skins
and prepare the forest beds
how the priests have cut their bodies with whips
how the bulls are led glistening like pools of oil
between the rows of worshippers.

EXODUS

From coastal towns,
where the sky innocently begins a hopeless journey,
came reports of unmarked stars
ruining schedules and confusing fishing-men;
and now it has come out
some northern weather-keepers
in their secret journals
recorded the arrangement of a new constellation;
but we were not told
and our streets seemed unchanged.

We knew nothing of Pharaoh's negotiations
or that higher powers were involved.
We went about our acts of charity,
visiting the city corners
where beggars calculated waltzes
and made rattles with pencils in a cup.
We paid all the lame and wired men
and gained the difficult gestures of many stumps.
We were loved those afternoons
by wagon-sitters and street-musicians:
we had numerous friends among the wretched.

Now our Nile has turned to blood
and in the cafes the scholars jest
about a cosmic wound.

Priests no longer smile
at our catalogue of charities
and even the beggars whom we pity and love
refuse our coins with a curse.

Councils have met and ministers
assure us of a clearer water.
Temples have given out
their beautiful warnings.
But what shall we do while the beggars
hate us from the corner,
regarding us like visitors
    who have come into their dark houses
and have seen too much,
or how shall we speak to our children
when they report each day
how their favorite animals have perished
in the city fountains.

My distant enemy in his linen tomb
still murmurs these questions through the
                    crumbling cloth,
though these children died in later battles
and the coloured feathers of their fountain
                    creatures
turned dust in the dynasties of war.
He still remembers the locusts
eating through the window panes
and the wooden carts

squeaking past the blackened castles
with their sad cargo of first-born dead.
And in his soft grave the shouts again are heard
as the walls of water break in on the chariots,
and under the terrible wave
go the beautiful boys from Memphis and Thebes
and the adorned riders charging against the
                                        foam.
Dream your questions, my oppressor, dream;
you of whom advice was never asked,
who did not order the attack,
whose tacit approval was always assumed.
You have endured your Flood
and you will have your Covenant:
perhaps now beneath the miles of water,
the Messenger, blessed be he,
moves between the alien chariots,
comforting Egyptian drowned
and teaching them songs for their damp harps:
how the sea did not wish to be a mouth,
how the east wind turned with grief to this
                                        calamity.

And I will instruct my friends
in your human innocence
as your seed and mine
gather in armies of blind giants
to war again at ancient useless borders;
and know, my taskmaster, that we too ask:
how long in the wilderness of Sinai

until the sons of bondsmen
understand their fathers' slavery;
who will read the chart of whip-scars on the backs;
who will interpret the numbers
burnt on our brothers' wrists.
And let this comfort you:
though no great fish came
to spit your drowning boys on dry land,
and no pillar of light illumined a road back
through the falling water,
still these uncommitted bodies
dried the swamp toward Jerusalem,
and your widows and sweethearts along the shore
wept a prayer which found our God.

BESIDE THE SHEPHERD

Beside the shepherd dreams the beast
Of laying down with lions.
The youth puts away his singing reed
And strokes the consecrated flesh.

Glory, Glory, shouts the grass,
Shouts the brick, as from the cliff
The gorgeous fallen sun
Rolls slowly on the promised city.

Naked running through the mansion
The boy with news of the Messiah
Forgets the message for his father,
Enjoying the marble against his feet.

Well finally it has happened,
Imagines someone in another house,
Staring one more minute out his window
Before waking up his wife.